E♭ ALTO SAXOPHONE

HOLIDAY FAVORITES

Solos and Band Arrangements
Correlated with Essential Elements® Band Method

Arranged by ROBERT LONGFIELD, JOHNNIE VINSON, MICHAEL SWEENEY and PAUL LAVENDER

Welcome to Essential Elements Holiday Favorites! There are two versions of each selection in this versatile book. The SOLO version appears in the beginning of each student book. The FULL BAND arrangement of each song follows. The ONLINE RECORDINGS or PIANO ACCOMPANIMENT BOOK may be used as an accompaniment for solo performance. Use these recordings when playing solos for friends and family.

PLAYBACK+
Speed • Pitch • Balance • Loop

To access audio visit:
www.halleonard.com/mylibrary

Enter Code
5139-8892-8180-6235

ISBN 978-1-5400-2792-4

HAL•LEONARD®

Visit Hal Leonard Online at
www.halleonard.com

00870010

Contact Us:
Hal Leonard
7777 West Bluemound Road
Milwaukee, WI 53213
Email: info@halleonard.com

In Europe contact:
Hal Leonard Europe Limited
42 Wigmore Street
Marylebone, London, W1U 2RN
Email: info@halleonardeurope.com

In Australia contact:
Hal Leonard Australia Pty. Ltd.
4 Lentara Court
Cheltenham, Victoria, 3192 Australia
Email: info@halleonard.com.au

AULD LANG SYNE

E♭ ALTO SAXOPHONE
Solo

Words by ROBERT BURNS
Traditional Scottish Melody
Arranged by MICHAEL SWEENEY

00870010

FELIZ NAVIDAD

3

Eb ALTO SAXOPHONE
Solo

Music and Lyrics by
JOSÉ FELICIANO
Arranged by PAUL LAVENDER

00870010

PARADE OF THE WOODEN SOLDIERS

Eb ALTO SAXOPHONE
Solo

English Lyrics by BALLARD MacDONALD
Music by LEON JESSEL
Arranged by PAUL LAVENDER

00870010

GOOD KING WENCESLAS

Eb ALTO SAXOPHONE
Solo

Words by JOHN M. NEALE
Music from PIAE CANTIONES
Arranged by ROBERT LONGFIELD

00870010

PAT-A-PAN
(Willie, Take Your Little Drum)

Eb ALTO SAXOPHONE
Solo

Words and Music by
BERNARD de la MONNOYE
Arranged by ROBERT LONGFIELD

SILVER BELLS

E♭ ALTO SAXOPHONE
Solo

**Words and Music by
JAY LIVINGSTON and RAY EVANS**
Arranged by PAUL LAVENDER

00870010

DO YOU HEAR WHAT I HEAR

E♭ ALTO SAXOPHONE
Solo

Words and Music by
NOEL REGNEY and **GLORIA SHAYNE**
Arranged by MICHAEL SWEENEY

From **THE SOUND OF MUSIC**

MY FAVORITE THINGS

E♭ ALTO SAXOPHONE
Solo

Lyrics by OSCAR HAMMERSTEIN II
Music by RICHARD RODGERS
Arranged by ROBERT LONGFIELD

00870010

From the Motion Picture Irving Berlin's HOLIDAY INN

WHITE CHRISTMAS

E♭ ALTO SAXOPHONE
Solo

**Words and Music by
IRVING BERLIN**
Arranged by JOHNNIE VINSON

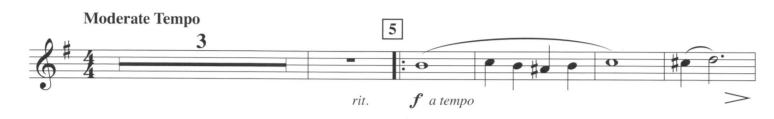

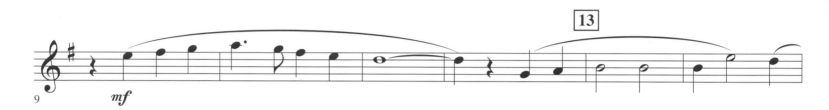

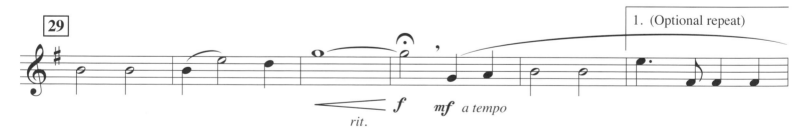

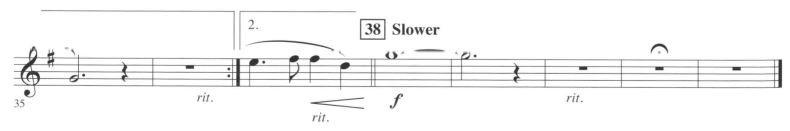

CHRISTMAS TIME IS HERE

Eb ALTO SAXOPHONE
SOLO

Words by LEE MENDELSON
Music by VINCE GUARALDI
Arranged by JOHNNIE VINSON

00870010

From Warner Bros. Pictures' THE POLAR EXPRESS

THE POLAR EXPRESS

E♭ ALTO SAXOPHONE
SOLO

**Words and Music by
GLEN BALLARD and ALAN SILVESTRI**
Arranged by JOHNNIE VINSON

AULD LANG SYNE

Eb ALTO SAXOPHONE
Band Arrangement

Words by ROBERT BURNS
Traditional Scottish Melody
Arranged by MICHAEL SWEENEY

FELIZ NAVIDAD

Eb ALTO SAXOPHONE
Band Arrangement

Music and Lyrics by
JOSÉ FELICIANO
Arranged by PAUL LAVENDER

PARADE OF THE WOODEN SOLDIERS

Eb ALTO SAXOPHONE
Band Arrangement

English Lyrics by BALLARD MacDONALD
Music by LEON JESSEL
Arranged by PAUL LAVENDER

00870010

GOOD KING WENCESLAS

Eb ALTO SAXOPHONE
Band Arrangement

Words by JOHN M. NEALE
Music from PIAE CANTIONES
Arranged by ROBERT LONGFIELD

PAT-A-PAN
(Willie, Take Your Little Drum)

E♭ ALTO SAXOPHONE
Band Arrangement

Words and Music by
BERNARD de la MONNOYE
Arranged by ROBERT LONGFIELD

SILVER BELLS

Eb ALTO SAXOPHONE
Band Arrangement

Words and Music by
JAY LIVINGSTON and RAY EVANS
Arranged by PAUL LAVENDER

DO YOU HEAR WHAT I HEAR

Eb ALTO SAXOPHONE
Band Arrangement

Words and Music by
NOEL REGNEY and GLORIA SHAYNE
Arranged by MICHAEL SWEENEY

00870010

From THE SOUND OF MUSIC

MY FAVORITE THINGS

Eb **ALTO SAXOPHONE**
Band Arrangement

Lyrics by OSCAR HAMMERSTEIN II
Music by RICHARD RODGERS
Arranged by ROBERT LONGFIELD

From the Motion Picture Irving Berlin's HOLIDAY INN
WHITE CHRISTMAS

Eb **ALTO SAXOPHONE**
Band Arrangement

Words and Music by
IRVING BERLIN
Arranged by JOHNNIE VINSON

00870010

CHRISTMAS TIME IS HERE

Eb ALTO SAXOPHONE
Band Arrangement

Words by LEE MENDELSON
Music by VINCE GUARALDI
Arranged by JOHNNIE VINSON

Moderately Slow, Smoothly

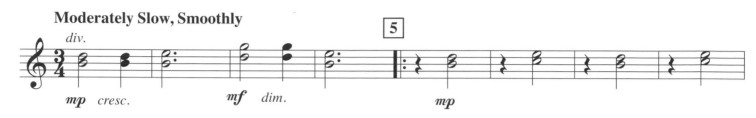

THE POLAR EXPRESS

E♭ ALTO SAXOPHONE
Band Arrangement

Words and Music by
GLEN BALLARD and ALAN SILVESTRI
Arranged by JOHNNIE VINSON